We All FALL Down

Written By
Alison L. Semler
Illustrated by: Marilyn Burt

We All Fall Down

Proofreading and Editing by Molly Whitman at Novel Mechanic
Illustrations by Marilyn Burt
Interior Book Formatting by AuthorTree

Independently published.

To Paxton- who inspired this book while learning to ride his bike.
To Presley- may this book inspire you to always get back up and try again.

Special thanks to my Aunt Marilyn for collaborating with me and creating characters that bring the story to life.

As the morning dew glistened, cold on the ground,
baby Deer decided to look around.

She stretched her neck and stood up tall,
never thinking she would stumble and fall.

But when she stepped one foot ahead,
her legs gave out and she fell instead.

"Ouch," cried Deer, as she lay there still.
"I can't do this, and I never will."

As Deer was about to give up
and go home,
she heard a sound,
and saw she wasn't alone.

Bunny hopped over and nudged her friend.
She looked at Deer and smiled and said,
"Don't give up, and please don't frown.
Remember Deer, we all fall down."

So Deer stood back up
with the strength she had.
She started to walk
and was feeling glad.

Bunny hopped all around,
happy to see the strength Deer had found.
"See," she said, glad she didn't quit.
"It takes a little practice, so just keep at it."

Deer and Bunny continued along,
but soon they heard a sad, crying song.

Quickly, they ran ahead to see what it could be.
Look! Their friend Owl had fallen out of his tree!

"Ouch," said Owl, as he started to cry.
"I jumped off my branch to see if I could fly."

"The wind blew hard, and then pushed me down.
I'll never do it! I guess I'll just stay here on the ground."

Owl stayed there, sad on the ground,
not even realizing his friends were around.

Deer walked over to help her friend.
She looked down at Owl and smiled and said,
"Don't give up and please don't frown.
Remember Owl, we all fall down."

So Owl spread his wings and leapt into the air.
He soon could fly from here to there.

Deer began to dance around,
happy to see the strength Owl had found.
"See," she said, glad he didn't quit.
"It takes a little practice, so just keep at it."

The three friends continued on their way to explore,
but froze when something let out a mighty roar.

They looked all around, just a little bit scared,
but quickly realized it was their friend, Bear!

“Ouch,” growled Bear, as he sat down with a sigh.
“I can’t climb this tree. It’s just way too high.”

Bear curled up in a big, fluffy heap,
and quietly to himself, he began to weep.

Owl flew over and nudged his friend.
He looked at Bear and smiled and said,
"Don't give up and please don't frown.
Remember Bear, we all fall down."

So Bear stood up and spread his arms wide.
Gripping the tree, he started to climb.

Higher and higher
to the top
where it's sunny,
and then down he came,
with a pawful of honey!

Owl began to flap around,
happy to see the strength Bear had found.
"See," he said, glad he didn't quit.
"It takes a little practice, so just keep at it."

The friends ate a snack as it began to get dark,
and were suddenly startled when they heard a loud bark.

They looked around slowly, and stood there in shock,
when out of bushes rolled their good friend Fox!

"Ouch," said Fox, as she began to moan.
"I can't get these berries, too sharp are the thorns."

Fox licked the cuts on the back of her tail,
but when her tummy growled, she started to wail.

Bear walked over and cleaned up his friend.
He looked at Fox and smiled and said,
"Don't give up and please don't frown.
Remember Fox, we all fall down."

So Fox stood up and shook off the dirt,
and went back to the bush, even though it hurt.
She gathered some food to bring back to her den,
but kept a few berries aside for her friends.

Bear began to jump around,
happy to see the strength Fox had found.
"See," he said, glad she didn't quit.
"It takes a little practice, so just keep at it."

As the sun went down and the moon shone bright,
the friends sat around the fire that night.
They told stories about their day,
and shared the food they collected along the way.

When they began to journey home,
they silently remembered they were never truly alone.
On days when they were feeling lost and sad,
they had friends to offer a helping hand.

When times seem hard and you happen to fall,
you are stronger than you think, after all.
Just don't give up and try not to frown.

Always remember,
We All Fall Down.

www.ingramcontent.com/pod-product-compliance
Ingram Content Group UK Ltd.
Pitfield, Milton Keynes, MK11 3LW, UK
UKHW060115300726
14090UKWH00002B/213

* 9 7 9 8 7 4 6 5 0 4 7 9 1 *